Jackie Robinson Breaks the Color Line

Andrew Santella

CHILDREN'S PRESS®
A Division of Grolier Publishing
New York • London • Hong Kong • Sydney
Danbury, Connecticut

Library of Congress Cataloging-in-Publication Data

Santella, Andrew.
    Jackie Robinson breaks the color line / by Andrew Santella.
        p.   cm.—(Cornerstones of freedom)
    Includes index
    ISBN 0-516-06637-4 (lib. bdg.) - ISBN 0-516-26031-6 (pbk.)
    1. Robinson, Jackie, 1919-1972—Juvenile literature.
2. Baseball players—United States—Biography—Juvenile literature.
3. Discrimination in sports—United States—Juvenile literature.
I. Title. II. Series
GV865.R6S26 1996
796.357'092—dc20
[B]   95-33636
                                 CIP
                                 AC

On the opening day of the 1947 baseball season, a Brooklyn Dodgers rookie stepped onto the field and forever changed the game of baseball. He didn't hit a home run that day, and he didn't win the game for his team. But he did make history. He did it by simply wearing the Dodgers uniform and playing baseball. The rookie's name was Jackie Robinson, and he was an African-American.

In the mid-1800s, some African-American, American Indian, and Latino ballplayers had appeared in professional games. But beginning in the 1880s, white professional players refused to play with and against non-whites.

Team owners, league officials, and even baseball's commissioners supported this racist tradition. So, until the 1920s, only white men could earn a living playing baseball in the United States.

From the late 1800s until 1947, major-league baseball teams were all white. This photo shows the all-white 1889 Boston Braves.

A 1924 team photo of the Kansas City Monarchs, one of the most famous Negro League teams

Branch Rickey

In 1920, the first professional baseball league for African-Americans began play. It was called the Negro National League. Soon, more leagues were established for black and Latino players. By the 1930s, the Negro Leagues (as they were called) showcased some of the most talented baseball players in the world. But these great players had to work for lower salaries and under worse conditions than white players in the major leagues.

One of the few baseball executives who sought to end segregation was Branch Rickey, general manager of the Brooklyn Dodgers. Rickey believed that racism had no place in America's national pastime. For years, he had ordered his scouts to watch out for the one special player who could break baseball's "color line" and become the first black player in the white major leagues. Rickey knew that the player to cross the color line would have to be an extraordinary person. He would need superior baseball talent to succeed on the field, of course. He would need tremendous courage to withstand the racism he surely would face. And he would have to be intelligent—smart enough to handle difficult situations. This player never could crack under pressure or break any of baseball's rules. If he were to fail in any way, he would fuel the arguments of those who supported segregated baseball. After years of searching, Branch Rickey had found the right man for the job—Jackie Robinson.

Jack Roosevelt Robinson was born on January 31, 1919, in the small town of Cairo, Georgia. He was the youngest of five children. After his father deserted the family, Jackie, his mother, and four siblings moved to Pasadena, California. Jackie's mother, Mallie Robinson, did housework for other families while working hard to keep her own family together. As they grew up, the Robinson boys became known as outstanding athletes. Jackie's brother, Mack, became one of the world's fastest sprinters. In 1936, he represented the United States in the Summer Olympic Games in Berlin, Germany. There, he finished second to Jesse Owens in the 200-meter dash.

Ironically, baseball was Jackie's worst sport in college. He was a star in football, basketball (below), and track-and-field (right).

In high school, Jackie participated in every sport that was offered, and he was usually the best player on his team. At Pasadena Junior College, he was just as versatile. A baseball scout remembered seeing Robinson leave in the middle of a baseball game and change uniforms to compete in the broad jump during a track meet. Then Jackie rushed back to the baseball field to continue playing in the baseball game. His incredible athletic talent earned him a scholarship to the University of California at Los Angeles (UCLA).

Robinson became the first student in UCLA history to earn varsity letters in four sports. He was the school's leading scorer in basketball and its best broad jumper. In football, he led the nation in rushing and in punt-return yards.

Jackie Robinson never graduated from UCLA. He was eager to make money to help support his mother, so he left school in 1941 to find a job. He worked at a youth camp and then played pro football in Hawaii for the minor-league Honolulu Bears. When the football season ended on December 5, 1941, a homesick Jackie Robinson immediately boarded a ship for California. Two days later, Japan attacked the U.S. military base at Hawaii's Pearl Harbor, and the United States entered World War II the next day. Within a few months, Robinson was drafted into the army.

Jackie Robinson was a versatile athlete in his youth; here he carries the ball in a football game.

Jackie Robinson entered the U.S. Army soon after Pearl Harbor was attacked by Japan.

Robinson was sent to Fort Riley, Kansas, for basic training. At Fort Riley and at his later post at Fort Hood, Texas, Robinson came face to face with racial injustice.

Robinson challenged military authority when he and other African-American soldiers were denied admission to Fort Riley's Officer's Candidate School, even though they met all the requirements. He also was dismayed by a lack of seating for black soldiers in Fort Riley's post exchange, where soldiers sometimes ate their meals. At Fort Hood, Robinson was riding a bus when the driver stopped the bus and demanded that Robinson move to the rear seats. In the 1940s, many communities required African-Americans to take seats at the back of buses, but this practice was illegal on army posts. Robinson refused to budge. When the bus arrived at his stop, Robinson was arrested by military police. He then faced a military court martial for disobedience.

After being put on trial by the army, Robinson was found not guilty of disobedience. He was honorably discharged from the army and returned home in 1944. But Robinson remained angry because he had been a victim of racial injustice even while training to fight for his country.

After leaving the army, Robinson decided to use his athletic skills to earn a living. He wanted to give baseball a try, but no major-league team would consider signing an African-American. So Robinson joined the Kansas City Monarchs, one of the best teams in the Negro Leagues.

Although the Negro Leagues were home to some of the world's best baseball players, the living and playing conditions were awful. To earn as much money as possible, teams often played two or even three games in a single day. They traveled in cramped, hot buses. They were barred from many restaurants and often obtained meals by waiting at the kitchen door to be fed leftovers and scraps. In most of the towns they visited, Negro League players were denied rooms in the good hotels. They sometimes slept on the floor in homes of local black families. Players even had to spend nights sleeping on the team bus.

Josh Gibson (below, scoring) was a legendary Negro Leagues player who never had the opportunity to play in the major leagues. He might have been a better slugger than Babe Ruth.

Jackie Robinson's stellar play on the field earned him a spot on the Negro National League All-Star team. His outstanding hitting, blazing speed, and sparkling fielding caught the attention of major-league scouts. Soon, Robinson received word that Branch Rickey of the Brooklyn Dodgers wanted to meet him.

In August 1945, Robinson traveled to New York to meet with Rickey. Robinson thought that Rickey wanted to hire him to play for the Brooklyn Brown Dodgers, the Negro League team Rickey supposedly was forming. Robinson quickly realized Rickey had something bigger in mind.

Rickey told Robinson that he wanted him to play for the major-league Brooklyn Dodgers. Rickey warned Robinson of the incredible stress he would face as the first African-American to cross baseball's color line. Racist white players and fans would taunt him, treat him unfairly, and scream insults at him from the moment he set foot on the field. Using graphic, offensive language, Branch Rickey shouted insults at Robinson, showing him what it could be like.

Robinson listened and grew angry. Finally, Robinson said, "Mr. Rickey, are you looking for a Negro who is afraid to fight back?"

Rickey replied, "Robinson, I'm looking for a ballplayer with guts enough *not* to fight back." Rickey explained that Jackie must prove his ability simply by playing baseball, not by getting involved in fights or shouting matches. If he was insulted, if pitchers threw at his head, if base runners spiked his legs, Robinson would have to turn the other cheek and walk away.

Robinson thought it over. He was not happy playing in the Negro Leagues for so little money. But he also felt uncomfortable with the prospect of having to keep quiet any time someone insulted him in the major leagues. Breaking the color line would be very difficult, but it was an opportunity he could not pass up. He accepted Rickey's challenge.

On October 23, 1945, the Dodgers announced the signing of Jackie Robinson. The first stop in his journey would be Canada. In 1946, Robinson played for the Montreal Royals, one of the Dodgers' minor-league teams. Robinson quickly proved that a black man could, indeed, compete with white players. In his first game for the Royals, Robinson hit three singles and a home run and stole two bases. Montreal fans immediately fell in love with Robinson's aggressive, sensational play. Robinson helped inspire his teammates as well, and the Royals dominated the International League.

Branch Rickey (second from left) looks on as Jackie Robinson signs his contract to play for the Montreal Royals.

Jackie is congratulated after slugging a home run in his first game as a Montreal Royal.

In other cities, Robinson did not receive a warm welcome. From Baltimore to Louisville, fans yelled racial slurs at him. In Indianapolis, he was kept from a game because a local law prohibited competition between the races. Pitchers threw at him to knock him down. "You never saw anything like it," one of his teammates said. "Every time he came up, he went down." In spite of this constant hostility, Robinson won the league batting title, and the Royals won the International League pennant.

After Robinson's successful year in the minor leagues, people began to wonder if he would be promoted to the Brooklyn Dodgers. But most of the baseball world attempted to block Robinson's promotion. In a vote of the sixteen baseball team owners, fifteen voted against Robinson joining the Dodgers—Branch Rickey was the only one to vote "yes." Baseball commissioner A. B. (Happy) Chandler, however, sided with Rickey and overruled the vote. Commissioner Chandler approved Robinson for the major leagues.

Dixie Walker

One of Robinson's biggest challenges would be winning the respect of his teammates and opponents. Several players stated publicly that they thought Robinson wasn't good enough for the big leagues. Dodgers star players Dixie Walker and Eddie Stanky circulated a petition protesting Robinson's presence at the Dodgers' spring-training camp in 1947. When Rickey heard about it, he called the white players into his office. He told them that Robinson was playing for the Dodgers whether they liked it or not. If anyone didn't like it, Rickey promised to get rid of *them*, not Robinson.

Ford Frick, president of the National League

Other teams also tried to stop Robinson from wearing a major-league uniform. Players for the St. Louis Cardinals tried to organize a league-wide strike to protest integration. National League president Ford Frick responded by threatening a lifetime ban from baseball on anyone participating in such a strike. "This is the United States," he said, "and one citizen has as much right to play as another."

Finally, opening day arrived. After weeks of protest and controversy, Jackie Robinson wore the Brooklyn Dodgers' uniform and became the first African-American player in the major leagues. His debut was not spectacular. He failed to get a hit in his first game. But his mere presence on the field was celebrated as a victory by millions of African-Americans across the nation.

It took several games before Jackie began displaying his athletic skills. His batting average stayed low, and he felt increasing pressure to produce. White fans screamed insults at him, pitchers threw at his head, and his family received violent threats in the mail. Robinson later wrote in his autobiography, "I had to fight against loneliness, abuse, and the knowledge that any mistake I made would be magnified because I was the only black man out there."

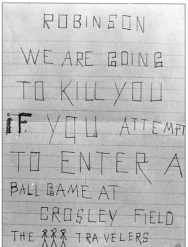

The author of this letter threatened to kill Robinson when the Dodgers played at Cincinnati's Crosley Field.

One team, the Philadelphia Phillies, treated Robinson viciously. During a three-game series, the Phillies and their manager, Ben Chapman, never stopped shouting abusive, racist insults at Robinson from the dugout. It is not unusual for baseball teams to try to distract opposing players (rookies especially) by shouting foul-languaged insults at them. But the Phillies were especially nasty to Robinson. And Jackie had promised Branch Rickey that he would not respond to this treatment.

It took several weeks before Robinson played up to his potential in the major leagues. Here, he is caught in a rundown by the Chicago Cubs.

Finally, during the last game of the Phillies series, Eddie Stanky became fed up with the barrage of insults. He shouted at the Phillies dugout, "Why don't you yell at someone who can answer back?" It was an important moment because Stanky had been one of the Dodgers who had organized the spring-training protest against Robinson. When the rest of the Dodgers saw Stanky stand up for Robinson, they all began to treat him as their teammate.

Robinson's performance gradually improved. With his lightning-quick baserunning and his daring, energetic playing style, the Dodgers and the rest of the league soon recognized that he definitely belonged in the majors. Robinson finished his first season with an excellent .297 batting average. He led the Dodgers in home runs (with twelve) and stole a league-high twenty-nine bases. He was named the National League Rookie of the Year. That year, the Dodgers played the New York Yankees in the World Series. Although the Dodgers lost, Robinson later said that playing in the Series was one of his greatest thrills.

Jackie Robinson's successful rookie season sent ripples of change throughout baseball. Larry Doby, a slugger for the Negro League Newark Eagles, broke the American League color line by playing for the Cleveland Indians in 1948. The Dodgers then signed Roy Campanella, formerly of the Baltimore Elite Giants. Campanella went on to become baseball's best catcher before he was crippled in an automobile accident.

Jackie Robinson developed a reputation as a daring and brilliant base runner.

Jackie Robinson and wife Rachel are presented with a new automobile in honor of his Rookie of the Year Award in 1947. Legendary entertainer Bill (Bojangles) Robinson presents Jackie Robinson with the car.

Jackie Robinson, himself, became an even bigger star. He won the National League batting title in 1949, earning Most Valuable Player honors. He played for the Dodgers for ten years and helped them win six National League pennants. By 1950, Robinson was the undisputed leader of the Dodgers. That year, his salary was $35,000. No other Brooklyn player ever had earned as much.

Ford Frick presents Robinson with the 1949 MVP Award.

JACKIE ROBINSON OPENED THE DOOR…

…and countless others followed. Thousands of minority athletes have thrived in the decades since Jackie Robinson's ground-breaking debut. It is now an everyday occurrence for African-American, Latino, and Asian athletes to play professional sports alongside white players. Here are some of the pioneers who left the Negro Leagues and followed Jackie Robinson across baseball's color line.

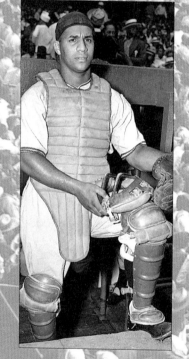

Larry Doby
Joined the Cleveland Indians in 1948 to become the first African-American player in the American League.

Roy Campanella
Joined the Brooklyn Dodgers in 1948 and became the best catcher in baseball.

Minnie Minoso
Native Cuban who played in the Negro Leagues before joining the Cleveland Indians in 1949; one of the first Latino stars in the major leagues.

Ernie Banks
Joined the Chicago Cubs in 1953 and slugged 512 home runs over the next nineteen years.

Frank Robinson
A Hall of Fame player for two decades. In 1973, Robinson was named player-manager of the Cleveland Indians, becoming the first African-American manager in the majors.

Willie Mays
Joined the New York Giants in 1951 and became perhaps the best all-around player in baseball history; hit 660 home runs in a twenty-two-year career.

Henry Aaron
Joined the Milwaukee Braves in 1954 and eventually became baseball's all-time home-run king with 755 homers.

As Jackie Robinson's fame grew, people began viewing him as a spokesman for other African-Americans. That sometimes put him in difficult positions. He was drawn into a dispute with civil rights leader Paul Robeson. Robeson had said that African-Americans should not fight in the United States military, because the government did not support civil rights for blacks. Robinson eventually traveled to Washington, D.C., to tell Congress that he and many other African-Americans disagreed with Robeson.

Jackie and Rachel Robinson arrive in Washington, D.C., where Jackie testified before Congress in 1949.

As Robinson grew older, his baseball skills began to decline. By 1955, he was not in the starting lineup every day, and he hit only .256. Still, the Dodgers made the World Series, giving Robinson one more chance to shine.

In the first game of the Series against the Yankees, Robinson did something that sparked his team. Standing on third base, Robinson charged down the line and stole home. It was a daring move for such an important game. Even though the Dodgers lost the game, Robinson had inspired the team, and they went on to win the World Series. It was the first championship in the team's history.

Jackie Robinson's thrilling steal of home plate helped inspire the Dodgers to win their first World Series championship. After years of frustration, they finally defeated the New York Yankees in 1955.

Still, Robinson knew that his baseball career was winding down. He began to prepare for retirement. Along with the rest of New York, Robinson was shocked when the team announced in 1957 that it was leaving Brooklyn for Los Angeles. Then the Dodgers traded Robinson to the Giants. But Jackie Robinson felt too much allegiance to the fans of Brooklyn to play for another team. Rather than play for the Giants, he retired from baseball.

Once his playing days ended, Robinson was determined to help change society for the better. He took a job as vice president of community relations with a coffee company called Chock

Already employed by the Chock Full o' Nuts coffee company, Robinson decided to retire from baseball rather than play for the Giants in 1957.

Full o' Nuts. He insisted that he be involved fully in the company's operation, not just a figurehead. He also headed fundraising efforts for the National Association for the Advancement of Colored People (NAACP). He helped to launch New York's Freedom National Bank and to establish its reputation for fairness toward minorities. Robinson helped it become one of the largest African-American-owned banks in the nation.

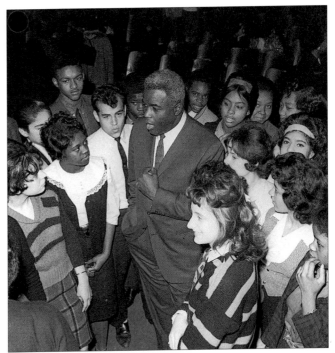

After retiring from baseball, Jackie Robinson was a visible and outspoken activist for African-Americans' civil rights. He participated in many protests for fair wages and workers' rights (top left) and spent hours talking with young people (top right). Robinson also found time to be with his wife and children (left).

In 1962, Jackie Robinson was elected to baseball's Hall of Fame. Not only had he been the first black player in the major leagues, he became the first black man to enter the Hall of Fame, baseball's greatest honor.

But in his middle age, Jackie Robinson also experienced loss and sadness. Branch Rickey, whom Robinson had grown to respect greatly, died in 1965. In 1968, his mother died while tending her garden in Pasadena. And his son, Jackie, Jr., returned from the war in Vietnam and developed a drug addiction he never overcame. The young man died in a car crash in 1971.

Branch Rickey (left) congratulates Jackie and Rachel Robinson at Robinson's Hall of Fame induction ceremony.

Robinson throws out the ceremonial first pitch at the 1972 World Series. This was his last public appearance before he died of a heart attack.

At the same time, Robinson's health was failing. In 1972, twenty-five years after he broke the color line, Robinson was honored with a ceremony before the first pitch of a World Series game. By the 1970s, major-league baseball was so fully integrated that more than half the players were African-American or Latino. But team managers, coaches, and front-office executives still were mostly white. Robinson addressed the crowd that night and said, "I will not be satisfied until I look over at that dugout and see a black manager leading a team."

Robinson never lived to see that day. He was suffering from diabetes and heart disease, and his eyesight nearly was gone. Soon after he was honored at the 1972 World Series, Jackie Robinson died of a heart attack at the age of fifty-three.

Eventually, African-Americans would manage major-league baseball teams. And, thanks to Robinson's example, they also had broken down barriers in other sports. When Robinson began playing for the Dodgers, most professional and college sports still were segregated. But in 1951, Chuck Cooper of the Boston Celtics became the National Basketball Association's first African-American player. In 1958, Althea Gibson became the first top-ranked African-American tennis player in the United States. And in 1963, Arthur Ashe became the first African-American to represent the United States in Davis Cup competition.

*Chuck Cooper (above) became the
first African-American player in the
National Basketball Association when
he joined the Boston Celtics in 1951.
In the 1960s, Arthur Ashe (left) helped
integrate tennis when he became
one of the sport's most dominant
champions. Ashe later wrote an
important series of books called*
A Hard Road to Glory. *The books
detailed the history of African-
Americans in sports.*

In the decades after Jackie Robinson broke baseball's color line, the civil rights movement gained momentum. The movement was spearheaded by Rev. Martin Luther King, Jr. (fourth from left).

In the years after Robinson broke the color line, African-Americans made great strides in securing their rights in American society. In the 1954 case of *Brown v. Board of Education,* the U.S. Supreme Court ruled that public schools could not be segregated. In 1955, an African-American woman named Rosa Parks refused to give up her bus seat in Montgomery, Alabama. Her action led to a highly publicized and successful boycott of Montgomery buses organized by Martin Luther King, Jr. Throughout the 1950s and 1960s, King spearheaded the revolutionary civil rights movement, which helped reverse countless racist, segregationist laws in the United States. The historic Civil Rights Act of 1964 outlawed segregation in public places and established fair voting rules for all races.

Jackie Robinson cleans out his locker after playing his last game as a Brooklyn Dodger.

Each of these events was a tremendous stride for civil rights in America. But one of the first steps in the civil rights movement was taken by Jackie Robinson in 1947. When he stepped onto the field in a Brooklyn Dodgers uniform, he was walking a path no African-American ever had been able to travel. The courage he showed in that moment and throughout his life changed American society forever.

GLOSSARY

Brooklyn Dodgers – National League baseball team that operated in Brooklyn, New York, until it moved to Los Angeles, California, in 1957

color line – policy that forbade African-Americans from playing professional baseball with white players

commissioner – head of an organization; the commissioner of baseball oversees all baseball players and team owners

court martial – a trial in which a member of the military is accused of a crime

Branch Rickey was a baseball executive

executive – an important business person; a baseball executive (a team president or general manager) is a non-player who helps make decisions for a team

figurehead – a person who holds an important job but who has no real power or responsibilities

Kansas City Monarchs – legendary team from the Negro National League

major leagues – the highest level of organized baseball in the United States; consists of the American and National Leagues

National Association for the Advancement of Colored People (NAACP) – organization that works to secure and protect the rights of African-Americans

Negro Leagues – baseball leagues that operated from the 1920s to the 1950s in which African-Americans and Latinos played professional baseball

Pearl Harbor – U.S. military base in Hawaii; after it was attacked by Japan in December 1941, the United States entered World War II

varsity letter – honor given to athletes who compete in sports in high school and college

World Series – the annual baseball championship series played by the champions of the American and National Leagues

Robinson earned a varsity letter in several sports

TIMELINE

Jackie Robinson born in Cairo, Georgia	**1919**
	1939
World War II {	**1942** Robinson enters the U.S. Army
	1944 Robinson discharged from army
	1945 Robinson joins Kansas City Monarchs
	1946 Robinson plays for Montreal Royals
	1947
	1949 Robinson is named National League Most Valuable Player
	1955 Robinson leads Dodgers to World Series title
	1957 Robinson retires from baseball
	1962 Robinson inducted into baseball's Hall of Fame
Jackie Robinson dies	**1972**
	1973
Henry Aaron breaks Babe Ruth's all-time home-run record	**1974**

April 10:
Robinson debuts with Brooklyn Dodgers, becoming first African-American player in major leagues

Frank Robinson becomes first African-American manager in major leagues

INDEX *(Boldface page numbers indicate illustrations.)*

PHOTO CREDITS

STAFF

Project Editor: Mark Friedman
Design & Electronic Composition: TJS Design
Photo Editor: Jan Izzo
Cornerstones of Freedom Logo: David Cunningham

ABOUT THE AUTHOR

Andrew Santella is a lifelong resident of Chicago. He is a graduate of Chicago's Loyola University, where he studied American literature. He writes about history, sports, and popular culture for several magazines for young people. He is the author of these other Children's Press titles: *The Capitol* (Cornerstones of Freedom) and *Mo Vaughn* (Sports Stars).